Benjamin Johnson Radford

History of Woodford County

Benjamin Johnson Radford

History of Woodford County

ISBN/EAN: 9783337326395

Printed in Europe, USA, Canada, Australia, Japan

Cover: Foto ©ninafisch / pixelio.de

More available books at **www.hansebooks.com**

OF

WOODFORD COUNTY.

GIVING A BRIEF ACCOUNT OF ITS SETTLE-
MENT, ORGANIZATION, PHYSICAL
CHARACTERISTICS AND
PROGRESS.

BY

B. J. RADFORD.

PEORIA, ILLS
W. T. DOWDALL, PRINTER, 117 MAIN STREET.
1877.

CONTENTS.

CHAPTER I.
	PAGE.
DESCRIPTION, NATURAL HISTORY AND EARLY SETTLERS.	7

CHAPTER II.
ORGANIZATION OF COUNTY. 22

CHAPTER III.
DOMESTIC AND SOCIAL LIFE. 29

CHAPTER IV.
AGRICULTURE AND FARM PRODUCTS. 40

CHAPTER V.
MANUFACTURES, TRADE, &C. 50

CHAPTER VI.
POLITICS, LAW AND MEDICINE. 57

CHAPTER VII.
EDUCATIONAL AND RELIGIOUS MATTERS. 67

PREFACE.

This brief account of the settlements and early life in Woodford County has been prepared under the auspices of the Old Settlers' Association. The information has been derived from many sources, and the accounts have sometimes been vague and contradictory, but it is believed that what is here recorded is reliable. There is no doubt much left out of this work which ought to be included, but it has been impossible to come at it. It would be well for all those who are in possession of facts and incidents, which would be useful in a revision of this history, to send them to Col. B. D. Meek, Chairman of the Committee for this work. Completeness and accuracy require that such a revision should be made as soon as it can be done thoroughly.

As before said, many have aided in gathering up what is here included, but especial mention should be made of Dr. Jas. S. Whitmire, John Clark, Dr. J. G. Zeller, Dr. A. Reynolds, Aaron Richardson, Peter Vance, Winton Carlock, John Summers, Jas. G. Bayne and Col. B. D. Meek, who have diligently assisted in hunting up facts and incidents.

May these pages call up pleasant reminiscences in the minds of the old, and stimulate the young to usefulness by their examples and their great successes in the face of difficulties and hardships.

B. J. RADFORD.

EUREKA, ILL., April 14, 1877.

A

HISTORY OF WOODFORD COUNTY.

CHAPTER I.

DESCRIPTION, NATURAL HISTORY AND EARLY SETTLERS.

Woodford County is very irregular in its boundaries, and the calculation of its area is somewhat difficult, but it contains not far from five hundred and fifty square miles. I have, with much care, calculated the geometric center of the county and find it to be somewhere in the northeast quarter of section twenty-two, in Roanoke township. The greater part of the county is prairie, the timber being confined chiefly to the bluffs and bottoms along water-courses. Much of the original timber has been cut away, but compensation has partly been made for this by the planting of groves and orchards upon the prairies. The favorite trees for these groves are black walnut and maple. Black locust promised much at one time, because of its rapid growth and excellent and durable wood, but about twenty years ago it was attacked by borers so vigorously that all the groves have been destroyed or rendered useless. The timber is found chiefly in the southern and western portions, along the Mackinaw and Illinois rivers and their tributaries. The other portions of the county are not only destitute of forests, but also of any considerable streams. Water for stock is usually obtained from wells, and can generally be secured at a depth varying from twenty to fifty feet, and for a few years past pumping by wind power has been becoming more and more general. Many valuable sorts of timber are natives of the county. Black, white, red and burr oaks are common; some black hickory and considerable white hickory. The black walnut and the wild cherry furnish very beautiful cabinet wood, which for beauty of marking, and fineness and richness of luster are excelled by nothing I have ever seen in our modern furniture warehouses; the sugar maple also furnishes a hard, durable and beautiful cabinet wood, as well as the ash, both of which are found in our forests. Red and white elms are common. Among other varieties may be mentioned cotton-wood, sycamore, mulberry, red-bud, crab-apple, plum, willow, hack-berry, sumac, hazel, dog-wood, elder, prickly-ash, &c. But the greater part of the county is prairie, and when first settled was destitute of trees or shrubs, and was entirely occupied by herbaceous vegetation. The chief part of this was grass, of a coarse sort, which went under the common names of prairie grass and slough grass. These were of vigorous growths, the culms, or flowering stalks, sometimes growing as high as seven or eight feet, and afforded excellent pasturage. There can be but little doubt that these natural pastures in Woodford County supported herds of bison, deer and other animals for centuries, nor are evidences lacking that our vast western prairies were inhabited by civilized people long before history began to be written. The grasses which grew in the sloughs and along the margins of the ponds were coarser and taller than those which grew on the uplands, and both localities were occupied by several varieties. There is very little of these native grasses now to be found in the county, and it is probable that the soil, having been cultivated, is rendered unfit for their production. The broad prairies were thickly interspersed with bright flowers, nodding their gay heads in the wind, as far as the eye could reach. Chief among these were those of the helianthus, or sunflower family. Flowers of this sort had a dark central head, surrounded by spreading rays of yellow or purple leaves, and were of many varieties. The ponds and sloughs were gorgeous with beautiful bright colored lilies, and many other species of wild flowers aided in ornamenting nature's broad flower garden—the prairies.

The burning of the prairies in the fall exposed the farms of the early settlers to much danger, and sometimes rendered travel dangerous if the wind was high. The tall, rank grass would be killed by the sharp frosts, and in a few days become dry and combustible. In a strong wind a billow of fire would sweep over the plain and lick up this grass with the speed of a race horse. Those who crossed wide prairies at such times of year usually carried some means of lighting a fire, and in case of need the grass was fired and a space soon burnt, which afforded a safe retreat from the approaching danger. Matches would have been a great boon, but there were no matches in those days. The early settlers were compelled to keep fire, or depend upon the somewhat uncertain supply of flint and tow. It was sometimes found necessary to send to a neighbor's and " borrow fire." The farmers would usually select some calm day, as soon as the grass would burn, and fire a strip about their fields, on the sides from which danger might be apprehended. Several neighbors would collect together, and all except one would be well armed with bundles of brush. The unarmed one would kindle a fire a few yards from the fence, and by means of brands conduct it in a line parallel with the fence. The men and boys with the brushes would arrange themselves close on either side of the fire line, and as soon as the burnt strip was wide enough to preclude all danger of being crossed by a fire coming in from the prairie, would whip out the flames, thus leaving a broad, black strip around the field. If this precaution was neglected the settler often paid pretty dearly for his carelessness. Many among us still remember the midnight alarm of the prairie on fire, and being hurried out of a comfortable nap to fight the destroying fiend. A praire-fire at night is a beautiful and fearful sight, and the roar of the flames may sometimes be heard for several miles. These are things of the past now, but it is well for our children to know the dangers and hardships through which their present comforts and conveniences have been brought to them.

The origin of our prairies has long been a puzzle and a subject for investigation and controversy among scientific men. It is evident that for ages the forests and prairies have lived neighborly, side by side, without either encroaching upon the other's territory. Why such different soils and products so close together? Many theories have been advanced to account for the treeless and shrubless character of the prairies. It has been asserted that the soil was too dry for trees; that it was too wet; that there was too much acid; that the prairies are the product of annual fires, which only permitted the growth of perennial grasses and annual herbs Nearly all are agreed, however, that our prairies were once the bottoms of extensive lakes and rivers, of which our ponds and sloughs are the lingering remnants, growing smaller and smaller as the country is raised. In Minnesota, among the numberless lakes, we perhaps see prairies in state of preparation, and much the same condition of affairs as prevailed in Illinois hundreds of years ago. This theory seems to carry with it the conclusion that the great lakes to the north and northeast of us once extended over a great portion of Illinois, and that Woodford County was a part of the bed of Lake Michigan. The theory also predicts that in time, if left to natural agencies, these great lake surfaces will become prairies, and a few little ponds and muddy sloughs their only vestiges. Before dismissing the subject of the prairies, it may be said that, evidently, the best preparation of prairie land for the planting of trees, is to break the clay subsoil by digging through it and filling in with some loose material that shall afford some sort of an artificial drainage.

Woodford County, geologically, is situated near the northern limit of the great Illinois and Missouri coal fields, which extend into Indiana, Kentucky, Kansas, Arkansas, Iowa and Minnesota. It reaches as far south as northern Texas, and probably covers an area of 100,000 square miles. Near the Illinois river the coal comes nearly to the surface, but on the prairies the profitable veins are from 300 to 600 feet from the surface, requiring deep shaft mining. Two attempts at mining of this character have been made, one at Minonk, and one near Metamora. The shaft near Metamora was sunk to the depth of 130 feet. At a little over fifty feet a seam of coal was found about one foot thick. At about 125 feet a three inch seam was met with, and at the bottom a seam about three feet and a half in thickness. Only about one-third of the thickness, in the middle, of this seam is good coal. A boring was made from the bottom of the shaft about 80 feet and no considerable coal found. The shaft at Minonk is nearly 600 feet in depth, and coal occurs as follows: at 325 feet a three-foot seam, which is evidently the one met with at the bottom of the shaft near Metamora. A very thin seam at about 380 feet, while at the bottom is found a seam of excellent coal nearly four feet in thickness. The uplands of the county have, everywhere, just beneath the soil, beds of diluvium or drift which will average almost a hundred feet in thickness. This is a most singular deposit and extends almost to the southern limits of the state. It is composed chiefly of yellow and blue clay with some sand and gravel. Imbedbedded in this material are rocks and boulders of all sizes and shapes, which have evidently been brought from a distance. It also abounds in fossils of plants and animals unlike anything now exisiting in this region. This singular mixture has been a great puzzle to geologists. It was first called *diluvium* because it was believed to have been caused by Noah's deluge; but this supposition was finally abandoned. It is now generally believed by geologists that all this material was brought, or *drifted*, here from some place further north. It is, therefore, now called " drift." The clays are sometimes called boulder clay because of the rocks distributed irregularly throughout them. The reasons cannot here be enumerated, but there are many for believing that this deposit was made by a great sea of ice, or glacier, which gradually crept down from the north, bringing with it these vast amounts of matter, and extending about as far south as the Ohio river.

The first comers found many sorts of animals here, which are at present nearly extinct. Among birds, there were quails, prairie hens and wild turkeys, all in great abundance, and all excellent for food. Many sorts of the feathered songsters are still with us, but their numbers have been too much thinned by useless and shameful warfare. Among our wisest laws are those for the protection of the birds. Snakes were plentiful, especially on the prairies, the largest species sometimes attaining the length of eight or ten feet. The most dreaded was the venomous rattlesnake, which was very common, but now, happily, is rarely seen. Stinging flies and mosquitoes were produced in countless numbers by the sloughs and ponds, and at certain seasons of the year were a vexatious pest to man and beast. A large bloodthirsty fellow, known as the "Green-head fly," drove an unceasing business during the latter half of the summer, and was an object especially dreaded by horses and cattle. They are about extinct now. Prairie wolves were numerous and familiar neighbors. They gave the early farmer nocturnal concerts, and paid themselves from his sheep pen, or his tender piglings. They seemed to be born dyspeptics and were always hungry. They would prowl in gangs, and it was unsafe for a man to be among them alone at night. One of the favorite methods of exterminating them was the circle hunt, and was conducted as follows: Upon a set day the settlers would gather at an appointed place on horseback; a captain was appointed and orders were given. As large a territory as practicable was enclosed and the game driven towards a central point, agreed upon before hand. When the game was finally penned by riders near together the work of killing begun. The wolves which escaped through the line were chased down and dispatched with clubs. Deer would also be often taken in the circle. Bounties were offered by the state for wolf scalps, and wolf hunting for a time became profitable. Money was scarce, and it was sometimes easier for the settler to get enough scalps to pay his taxes than enough money. The poor wolf has about succumbed to this unceasing warfare, and we have seen his lank, familiar visage for almost the last time. To his old neighbors and acquaintances this is a matter of small regret, which argues that Canis Lupus was a bad citizen. There was a few foxes and many deer which afforded sport in the way of the chase. Deer and fox hounds had then some excuse for existence, but now their occupation is gone. The groves abounded in squirrels, and raccoons were common. Coon hunting was chiefly prosecuted at night, and was splendid sport for boys and dogs. A fight between a large "coon" and the dogs was an exciting and interesting spectacle. A wise old cur who knew how to kill a coon, enjoyed an enviable reputation among the boys and his canine associates. A good "coon dog" was an important member of the family. Many an inexperienced cur got the conceit taken out of him by a short tussle with a full grown raccoon. Badgers' were occasionally met with, and now and then a black bear or a panther. Wild cats and skunks, and other animals common to the Mississippi Valley, were here. As before said, most of these creatures, little and big, are fast becoming extinct, and it would be useful in aftertime to have carefully prepared specimens of them all. It should be part of the work of our public schools to collect, classify, name and preserve all these objects. The numbers of wild animals were greatly diminished by the deep snow of the winter of 1830-1. This snow began Dec. 27, 1830, and fell to the depth of three or four feet, and lay on the ground until vast numbers of animals perished.

There were a few Indians in the county at the time of settlement by the whites, but the two races did not come into conflict to any extent. The advancing wave of civilization seemed to follow up the retreating wave of barbarism. The first settlers encountered a few Indians, chiefly Pottawotomies, and in 1832 were involved to some extent in the Black Hawk war, but the active operations were further north than Woodford County. A number of the early settlers were engaged in this war, some of whom are still living among us. This war is remarkable for the fact that both Abraham Lincoln and Jefferson Davis were engaged against Black Hawk.

The poor Sac Chief little thought that he was waging war with palefaces who would become so much greater chieftains than himself.

The first white man who settled in the limits of this county was one Bleylock, who was found in the river bottom, near Spring Bay, as early as 1819. A few years after this, pioneers began to make settlements here and there, but the number did not increase very rapidly till about 1835. I have endeavored to collect the names of settlers in the various neighborhoods up to this date, and the result will be found in the following table. It includes all those who located in the county previous to 1836, so far as could be ascertained, but no doubt there are some whose names do not appear here:

HISTORICAL TABLE.

NAMES.	DATE.	LOCALITY.	REMARKS.
Wm. Blanchard	1822	Near Spring Bay	Farmer, came to Peoria in 1819.
—Dillon	....	" "	Farmer, erected corn mill in 1827.
Horace Crocker	1831	" "	Farmer, erected flouring mill in 1828.
Phinneas Shottenkirk	1831	" "	do
Joseph Belsley	1829	" "	do
Richard Williams	1835	" "	do
William Hunter	1834	" "	do
John Snyder	1834	" "	do
Isaac Snyder	1834	" "	do
Peter Snyder	1834	" "	do [hunting and fishing.
David Snyder	1819	" "	Found by first settlers living Indian fashion,
Wm. (or Geo.) Bleylock	1824	" "	Miller and chair maker.
John Stephenson	1829	" "	Farmer
Jesse Dale	1828	" "	do
Joseph Crocker	1829	" "	Kept a ferry at the "Narrows."
David Matthews	1828	" "	Farmer.
Jacob Wilson	1829	" "	do
"Widow" Donahue	1829	" "	do
George Hopkins	1829	" "	do
Hiram Curry	1824	" "	do
Austin Crocker	1823	" "	Afterwards settled near Metamora.
Geo. Kingston	1827	" "	Farmer.
Charles Fielder	1823	" "	do
Wm. Phillips	1833	" "	do built a mill on Partridge Creek.
Louis Guibort	....	" "	do
—Gingerich	1830	" "	do and miller.
Wm. Hoshor	1833	Near Germantown	do and Methodist pioneer preacher.
Zedick Hall			

HISTORICAL TABLE—CONTINUED.

NAMES.	DATE.	LOCALITY.		REMARKS.
Samuel Bock	1834	Near Germantown	Farmer.	
Thomas Sunderland	1834	"	do	
John Sharp	1830	"	do	
Charles Molitor	1835	"	do	
Peter Muler	1832	"	do	
John F. Smith	1830	"	do	[of Jos. Meek, 1825.
Joseph Dillon	1824	In Walnut Grove	do	broke first land in neighborhood on farm
Charles Moore	1826	"	do	
Daniel Meek	1826	"	do	
Wm. Atteberry	1829	"	do	
John Davidson	1829	"	do	
John Dawdy	1829	"	do	
Joseph Meek	1830	"	do	
Henry Meek	1830	"	do	
John Bird	1827	"	do	
—— Wathen	1827	"	do	
Joshua Woosley	1831	"	do	school teacher and Christian preacher.
Jonathan Baker	1826	"	do	
Wm. Bird	1830	"	do	
Joseph Martin	1829	"	do	
Mathew Bracken	1829	"	do	
James and Robert Bird	1829	"	do	and miller.
Francis Willis	1831	"	do	
Wm. R. Willis	1834	"	do	practiced medicine some.
James Mitchell	1833	"	do	
Daniel Travis	1831	"	do	
Solomon Tucker	1835	"	do	practiced dentistry some.
Wm. Davenport	1835	"	do	Christian preacher, practiced law some.

HISTORICAL TABLE—CONTINUED.

NAMES.	DATE,	LOCALITY.		REMARKS.
Caleb Davidson	1831	In Walnut Grove	Farmer.	
David Deweese	1830	"	do	
Thomas Deweese	1830	"	do	
John Oatman	1830	"	do	
John Butcher	1831	"	do	
Cooley Curtis	1831	"	do	
Benj. J. Radford	1834	"	do	
Mathew Blair	1830	"	do	
Ben Major	1833	"	do	preacher and practiced medicine some.
Elijah Dickinson	1835	"	do	
M. R. Bullock	1834	"	do	
Jas. Harlan	1832	South of Walnut Grove	do	
Daniel Allison	1831	" " "	do	
Isaac Black	1831	Walnut Grove	do	
Thomas Bullock	1835	"	do	
Nathan Owen	1829	"	do	
Thos. Deweese	1833	"	do	
Thomas Kircade	1833	"	do	
Josiah Moore	1830	Panther Creek	Farmer and miller.	
Campbell Moore	1830	"	Farmer and miller.	
Amos Watkins	1830	"	do	and Christian preacher.
Warren Watkins	1830	"	do	
Amasa Stout	1828	"	do	
Eli Patrick	1829	"	do	
Allen Patrick	1829	"	do	
Jas. S. McCord	1830	"	da	
Thos. A. McCord	1830	"	do	
Aaron Richardson	1831	"	do	

HISTORICAL TABLE—CONTINUED.

NAMES.	DATE.	LOCALITY.		REMARKS.
James M. Richardson	1831	Panther Creek	Farmer	
Joseph Wilkerson	1832	"	do	
Noel Meek	1832	"	do	school teacher.
Basil Meek	1832	"	do	
John Armstrong		"	do	
Wm. C. Moore	1828	"	do	
—— Bilberry		"	do	
Adam Heathorne		"	do	and Christian preacher.
James Robeson	1835	"	do	
James Rayburn		"	do	
Wm. McCord	1831	"	do	
E. Dixon	1835	On the Mackinaw	Miller.	
Gershom Harvey	1825	" "	Farmer.	
Robert Phillips	1828	White Oak Grove	do	
Samuel Phillips	1828	"	do	
Lewis Stephens	1830	"	do	
Jas. V. Phillips		"	do	
Samuel Kirkpatrick	1831	"	do	
Jonah Brown	1833	"	do	
Jacob Ellis		"	do	
James Vance	1835	"	do	
Abner Peeler		"	do	school teacher and Christian preacher.
Reuben Carlock	1833	"	Settled in Dry Grove in 1827, farmer.	
Winton Carlock	1833	"	Farmer.	
Lewis Stover	1832	"	do	and Christian preacher.
—— Saudifer		"	do	
John Harbert	1829	"	do	
John Benson	1831	"	do	

HISTORICAL TABLE—CONCLUDED.

NAMES.	DATE.	LOCALITY.		REMARKS.
Wm. Benson	1831	White Oak Grove		Farmer
Jas. Benson	1831	" " "		do
Wm. Sowards	1823	Near Metamora		do
Solomon Sowards	1823	" "		do
George Kingston	1825	" "		do
David Banta	1831	" "		do
Cornelius Banta	1831	" "		do
John Page	1834	" "		do
Peter Engle	1833	" "		do
John Verkler	1833	" "		do
Humprey Leighton	1835	" "		do
C. P. Mason	1835	" "		do
Benj. Williams	1827	Near Partridge Creek		do
Christian Smith	1833	" " "		do
Morgan Buckingham		Near Low Point		do
Thomas Jones	1834	" " "		do
Jas. Owen	1834	" " "		do and Christian preacher.
Isaac Moulton	1835	" " "		do
Parker Morse	1835	" " "		do

CHAPTER II.

ORGANIZATION OF COUNTY.

For about fifteen years after their first settlement the localities, mentioned in the first chapter, were included in the boundaries of McLean and Tazewell counties, the dividing line between the two running north and south through the present town of Eureka. Up to this time settlements had been made near the timber and along the water-courses in all parts of the present territory of the county, but the prairies were unoccupied. Some places acquired considerable importance, in the early times, which are at present almost abandoned. Bowling Green was a thriving village, where goods were sold, and shops were established; she also possessed her share of professional men. Her streets were named in honor of the then chief cities of Illinois: Chicago, Peoria, Springfield, Danville and Bloomington. Versailles was laid out with much care. The streets at the four boundaries were called, respectively, North, West, South and East, whilst the intermediate ones had such appropriate titles as Peoria, Chestnut, Bloomington, Walnut, State and Locust. The settlement at Metamora was called the settlement of Partridge Point. It was afterward called Hanover, and finally Metamora. El-Paso, Eureka, Minonk, Secor and Roanoke were unborn, and there was little to indicate that these would ever be centers of population and trade. Not many of the younger portion of our people would know where to locate Ross's Point or Travis's Bridge. Yet these were formerly places of great note, and I find Travis's Bridge now near Mt. Zion church, in Cruger township, mentioned in the legislature of 1840 as one of the important and well known places in the state.

By the year 1840 settlers had become numerous, and it began to appear that new counties must be formed for the convenience of the people. Both McLean and Tazewell counties were very large and many of the settlers remote from the places of holding courts. A few men about Versailles, under the leadership of Thomas Bullock, Sr., made an effort in 1840 to secure the formation of a new county, with Versailles as the seat of justice. A petition to the legislature was prepared and circulated. There was a movement at Washington about the same time to form a new county with Washington as the county seat. Most of the settlers on the west side of Walnut Grove, then Tazewell county, favored the latter project. Uncle Tom Bullock got information of the plans of the Washington men, and with great energy pushed the circulation of his petition and as soon as possible laid it before the legislature. The other party, finding themselves too slow, were compelled to take the defensive, and soon appeared with a remonstrance. Excitement ran pretty high, and the journals of the two houses show that the bill for the formation of Woodford County had a long and doubtful embryonic period. It was frequently called up and advocated or opposed, tinkered and half-soled, and then "referred." Attempts were made to have the proposition submitted to a vote of the inhabitants of the territory to be organized into the new county. But on the twenty-seventh day of February, 1841, the bill was finally approved by the governor without such submission. It was entitled, an Act for the formation of the County of Woodford, and I suppose this name was selected by Uncle Tom Bullock to perpetuate the remembrance of his old county in Kentucky. The first section of the act describes the boundaries as follows: "Beginning at the southwest corner of Livingston county, thence on a straight line to the northwest corner of the southwest quarter of section twenty, township twenty-five north, range one east of the third principal meridian; thence south to the northwest corner of the southwest quarter of section twenty-nine, township and range aforesaid; thence west to the Tazewell county line; thence north one and a half miles; thence west to the center of township twenty-five north range two west, of the third principal meridian; thence north to the line between townships twenty-six and twenty-seven; thence west to the Illinois river; thence with said river to the northwest corner of Tazewell county; thence with the northern boundary of Tazewell and McLean counties to Livingston county; thence south to the place of beginning."

The second secton provides for the election of county officers, on the second Monday of April, 1841. The election was to be held at Versailles and the places for voting for Justices of the Peace in the county. The third section provides that the poll-books shall be returned to Versailles, to Matthew Bracken, John W. Brown and Morgan Buckingham, three Justices of the Peace. Section four assigns Woodford County to the eighth judicial circuit, and directs the judge thereof to appoint a Circuit Clerk and hold courts therein as soon as organization is effected. Sections five, six and seven provide for the disposition of suits begun previous to organization ; the jurisdiction of officers already elected, and the proper disposition of the school fund. The eighth section locates the seat of justice at Versailles for two years, upon the condition that the inhabitants should provide a good and suitable building for courts and other public business ; and directs an election to be held at the end of the two years for a permanent location of the seat of justice. The place chosen must receive a majority of all the votes polled, and give security for a donation of at least fifteen hundred dollars for erection of county buildings. Section nine fixes the share and the time of payment of the McLean county debt, by those who had been citizens of that county ; and the tenth and last section places Woodford in the same senatorial and representative district with McLean and Tazewell.

On the 17th of February, 1843, the legislature passed an act to add to Woodford County all that part of Tazewell lying north of the line dividing townships twenty-five and twenty-six, north ; with the proviso that the annexation should be approved by a majority of the legal voters of each county. A special election was held in both counties, but it seems the measure was not adopted. This addition would have given us Washington, and possibly have given Washington the county seat. On the 28th day of February, 1843, the line between Woodford and McLean counties was permanently established, as follows: " beginning at the southwest corner of Livingston county, running thence west three miles, thence south six miles, thence west three miles, thence south two and a half miles, thence west three miles, thence south one mile, thence west one and three-quarters miles, thence south one mile, thence west one-fourth of a mile to the corner of Woodford County." This constitutes the present boundary.

According to section nine of the original act forming Woodford County, those who had been citizens of McLean county were, after 1844, to pay twelve hundred dollars of the McLean county debt. On the 1st day of March, 1843, the legislature repealed this section, and thus relieved the citizens of this obligation.

It had been provided by the original act that after two years the seat of justice should be permanently located by an election to be held at the usual places of voting in the county; but on the 28th day of February, 1843, this part was repealed by an act appointing James K. Scott, of DeWitt, Joseph L. Sharp, of Fulton, and John H. Harris, of Tazewell, a commission for the purpose of locating the county seat of Woodford County. These commissioners were to meet at Versailles on the first Monday in June, 1843. They were to be duly sworn and locate the seat of justice upon the faithful consideration of "geographical boundaries, convenience of inhabitants," present and prospective settlements, eligibility of situations and such other rights as they might think proper. The act further provides that when the said commissioners shall have made the location of the seat of justice they shall make report thereof to the County Commissioners' court, who shall make due record thereof, and direct the application of the donation required in the original act. On the sixth of March following a supplemental act was passed appointing Levi A. Hannaford, of Peoria, and John H. Bryant, of Bureau, additional commissioners to act in conjunction with those already appointed. This commission located the county seat at its present situation, and the necessary steps were soon taken by the County Commissioners to erect public buildings, which are those in use at present.

As we have already said, the formation of Woodford County was chiefly due to the efforts of Thos. Bullock, Sr., and through his influence Versailles enjoyed the distinction of being the capital for two years. The "good and suitable building" required by the legislature for the public business seems to have been promptly furnished, and I am informed that it still rears its venerable gables in the neighborhood, being used as a barn. In this building, in September, 1841, was held the first circuit court in Woodford County. Judge Samuel H. Treat was on the bench, and among the attorneys at this first session were Abraham Lincoln, the gallant Col. Ed. D. Baker, David Davis, Stephen T. Logan, Jno. J. Harding, Jno. T. Stewart and A. Gridley.

The first county officers were as follows: Jos. Meek, Josiah Moore and James Boys, County Commissioners, and John J. Perry, Clerk of county commissioners court and Recorder; J. B. Holland, Judge of Probate S. S. Parke, Surveyor; S. J. Cross, Circuit Clerk; Wm S. Magarity, Sheriff; William Hoshor, Coroner; Jas. S McCord, Treasurer; Joshua Woosley, Assessor, and W. R. Rockwell, Collector. The political organization as effected above remained till 1850, when the present township organization was adopted, after much discussion, excitement and speech-making, and strenuous opposition. The county commissioners have been superseded by the board of supervisors, and other changes effected not necessary to be enumerated here. The county at present comprises seventeen townships.

CHAPTER III.

DOMESTIC AND SOCIAL LIFE.

The progress which Woodford County has made in civilization can be traced no more plainly in any respect than in the conveniences, appointments and methods of domestic life. From a domestic condition differing but little from that of the Indian, a change has been made to the comfort, elegance and luxuriousness of the highest and most artificial civilization in a single generation. The first settlers of the county dwelt in log cabins of rude and hasty construction. No lumber was to be had. Saw-mills had not been erected, and the pine lumber, now so common, was unheard of. Many of the cabins contained but a single room; and a double one, of two rooms, was a luxury many a family could not afford. The matter of ventilation, of such serious consideration in modern architecture, gave them but little trouble, except, perhaps, that it was a little too easy of accomplishment. The logs of which the house was built were sometimes hewed, so as to present a smooth surface on both sides of the wall, but often they were notched and laid up hastily; the pressing needs of the settler's family not permitting the hewing to be done. The cracks, of irregular shape, between the logs were filled with clay, made into a sort of plaster. If the domicile was so pretentious as to display window-lights they were made of oiled paper. The doors and floors were made of puncheons, or rough boards, split from trees and battened together with wooden nails or pegs. The roof was covered with clap-boards, or sometimes thatched. The heating apparatus was the fireplace with its bright, hospitable face. The chimney was built of split sticks, piled up in a rectangle, pen fashion, and plastered inside and out with clay mud. Wooden pegs, driven into the wall, or clap-board shelves resting upon pegs, answered the purpose of wardrobe, cupboard and bureau. Tables, benches and bedsteads were of such rude construction as the skill and implements (usually an ax and an augur, with a hunting knife or jack knife) of the pioneer could effect.

When we come to consider the culinary arrangements of these old-time households we are sensible of occupying a comfortable vantage ground. We need not remove from the parlor or sitting room to find the objects of our investigation. The same apartment often served for the parlor, dining room, library, kitchen, cellar, storehouse and bedroom. There were no cooking stoves in those days. The meals were prepared at the fireplace. Sometimes, for lack of vessels, the bread and potatoes were baked in the ashes, while the meat was roasted on a spit, or twig held over the fire by hand. The well-to-do settlers had ovens, pots, kettles, frying pans, &c. Corn bread was usually baked in hot ashes and coals, without vessel of any sort. For baking biscuits a round, shallow oven was used. It was of iron, and tolerably thick. The biscuits were placed in the oven which was set upon the coals in front of the fireplace. A heavy lid was placed upon the vessel and a shovel-full of coals on top of that. The biscuits were then subjected to heat from both sides, and came out nice and light. I remember to have seen among the old residents an apparatus for baking thin cakes from batter. These cakes were very toothsome, and were called waffles. Waffle-irons were made of two rectangular pieces of iron, about six by eight inches, which fitted together in such way as to form a mold, or matrix, which would make a cake about half an inch thick. Each half of the mold was attached to an iron rod three or four feet long. These rods were pivoted together near the molds, and the irons were opened and shut scissors-fashion. The batter being put in the waffle-iron was thrust into a hot place in the fire, and in a few seconds there was turned out a sweet and beautifully indented waffle. The modern pancake is a degenerate and sorry descendant of this cherished ancestor.

Fruits were stewed for immediate use, or made into pies. For winter they were jammed or preserved. Both processes were very expensive on the account of the scarcity of sugar; and a small quantity of such delicacies was stored carefully away to be produced only on extra occasions. The modern processes of canning fruit were unknown; apples were not yet being produced, and the long winter's subsistence consisted chiefly of bread and meat. Many a lad was rejoiced at the advent of some distinguished visitor, because of the probability afforded thereby of seeing, and possibly tasting, a little preserves. Vegetables, pumpkins and hominy were cooked in pots or kettles, set over the fire. After a time an improvement was adopted in the shape of a long iron arm, fastened to an upright iron rod attached to the jamb in such way as to turn readily in any direction. This arm could thus be turned so as to bring a pot suspended from it over the fire or back against the jamb, out of the way. This was called a crane, and was considered a wonderful convenience. Cooking stoves did not come into general use until near 1850, the first having been introduced about ten years before.

Before apples were to be had the staple fruit was the golden and classic pumpkin. The pumpkins were pared and cut into pieces of convenient size for drying. They were then run upon strings and hung up along with red pepper pods, seed corn and jerked venison, articles at once useful and ornamental in the settler's homely cabin. Crab-apples were sometimes gathered and buried in the ground for winter use. Walnuts, hickory and hazel nuts were abundant, and the younger fry subsisted largely upon these. In the way of flesh the pioneer's family was usually well supplied. In addition to the domestic animals and fowls, which were soon introduced, the country abounded in excellent game, as mentioned elsewhere, and the Mackinaw, Walnut and Panther creeks were full of choice fish. Milk and butter soon came to be plenty, but tea and coffee were costly and rare luxuries. Wild bees were plentiful, and many a hollow tree furnished the early settler with delicious honey.

Among the early settlers store-clothes were out of the question. The garments, as well as the fabrics of which they were made, were the products of home industry.

These fabrics were linen, jeans and linsey. The linen was prepared from the flax, raised and manufactured by the rude implements then at hand. The breaking, hatcheling, spinning and weaving of flax, with their poor facilities, was a slow and laborious work for our fathers and mothers, and a nice piece of home-made linen was an article of great value. Linsey was made of linen, or usually cotton, chain with fine woolen filling. This constituted the chief winter wear of the women. Jeans was made in much the same manner, except that the filling was heavier than for linsey. It was usually colored brown with walnut bark, or rendered more beautiful and expensive with the familiar blue dye. A well fitting suit of linsey or blue jeans was both handsome and durable, and there was a laudable emulation among housewives to produce the best and prettiest fabrics of this sort. The wool for these fabrics was either dyed before carding or in the hank. The settler would shear his flock about the beginning of summer, and the wife and children would put in their spare time preparing the winter apparel during the season. Before the establishment of carding mills, which was about the year 1831, the whole process of preparing wool was carried on at home. The first thing to be done with the wool, after being thoroughly cleansed, was to card it. The cards consisted of two thin boards, about four inches wide and one foot long, thickly set on one side with fine, short bent wires; at the side of each was attached a short handle. With a pair of these instruments an accomplished lady of the period could quickly and skillfully work a pile of snowy wool into smooth, even rolls. These rolls were then spun into threads, which were reeled into hanks. the yarn was then twisted by means of the spinning wheel, and run upon "quills." The thread was then ready for the loom. After the materials were ready an expert weaver could produce five yards of jeans in a day. Some of the earliest settlers wore buckskin clothing, but this never prevailed to any extent in Woodford County.

The social customs among the early comers were of the most natural and unostentatious sort. Hospitality was a marked characteristic of the times. Gatherings were frequent, and visiting a feature of social life much more general than at present. Personal social equality was secured by the necessary equality in circumstances and belongings. Social distinctions, in our best civilizations, do not depend upon ability and character so much as upon differences in personal surroundings. Houses, furniture, vehicles and dress are the props upon which the social grades of christendom are built. Among our fathers and mothers all were alike in these respects, and the personal equality, which gave so much zest and pleasure to social life, was a matter of course The desire to excel in dress and domestic appointments, which it is useless to deny is the sin and bane of modern society, was never awakened in the hearts of our pioneers. Circumstances made it impossible, and left room for the exercise of their kindly and social instincts, and, no doubt, gave them purer and sweeter springs of social enjoyment than are now accessible. Long and frequent visits among neighbors were prompted and hospitality quickened not solely by charity, though this in large measure must be conceded to the early settlers. The common and stereotyped invitation to "come and spend the day," and the often acceptance thereof, were prompted somewhat by the same instinct which led the Athenians to spend their time in hearing and telling some new thing. Visits and social gatherings were the occasions of hearing and telling the news. A stranger was received and entertained over night, without charge, partly from the same motive which prompts a man to buy a newspaper or a story book. Nor is this curiosity a mean or useless thing. It impels to those investigations of history and nature which are constantly enlarging the bounds of our knowledge. Among the early settlers these things gave point, interest and dignity to fireside conversation ; but the news of to-day has largely deserted social channels, and become an article of commerce, leaving to neighborly and social intercourse the emptiness and nonsense so wearisome and disgusting to men of sense. The good old fireside talks of the early life are a thing of the past. The matter and motive of them are found elsewhere, and, so far as this generation is concerned, conversation is almost a lost art. That it will be revived upon a different basis now being laid in universal education can scarcely be doubted.

In the way of gatherings there were house raisings, weddings, funerals, elections, spelling matches, religious meetings and parties. It was a duty no settler thought of shirking to help his neighbor to raise his house or barn. These were constructed of heavy materials, and the appliances were very rude. It was heavy and dangerous work, and the raising of a large barn required the united energies of a whole community. The early elections were not by ballot, as now, but each voter signified his candidate or candidates to the office *viva voce*. This prevented the secresy and quiet now possible, and an election was a lively and interesting occasion. Weddings were not the solemn and stately things of the present; but occasions of the utmost fun and festivity. A funeral was a time of sadness Each member of a small community possessed a larger importance than the dweller in a large city, or dense population. The early settler looked upon the loss of a member much as a family does at the loss of a brother or sister· There were no beautiful and guarded cemeteries. The loved one was laid to rest on the lone hill-side in the forest, encased in a rude coffin, made of boards split from a tree. There were no burial cases—none of those innocent deceptions by which we persuade ourselves that we keep something of our lost ones to ourselves, and rescue the precious clay from corruption. It was a literal returning of dust to dust, and could not be other than sad. Spelling matches were a useful means of education, but were engaged in perhaps more from the enjoyment they afforded, and the sparking facilities enjoyed by the youngsters, than from any sense of their utility. Religious meetings were at first held in private houses, and were thus semi-domestic in character, and it is a matter of regret that along with the meeting there has been too much of a tendency to banish to the meeting house the worship and piety which should have been partly retained at home. Parties were usually given over to the young people, and the boys and girls generally managed to have a good time ; a little uproarous sometimes with "hurly-burly," "spin the plate," or "weevilly wheat," but, nevertheless, enjoyable and innocent. There has been considerable change in the matter of amusements and pastimes. The immense amount of work to be done did not allow of so much leisure as may be enjoyed now, but yet there would be many seasons which could be spared to fun and recreaation. One of the chief sports, half fun and half business, was hunting. Every settler possessed a rifle, and often each boy must have one, and the cabin would be ornamented by several of these weapons upon their hooks. Even now you may find, in the old farm houses, many a long, trusty rifle which did its share in the early day, in supporting the family. There it hangs idly in its rack, and quickens the recollection of the old man in the scenes and enjoyments of the days that can return no more. It seems to have outlived its usefulness, but well deserves a place in the family archives for what it has done. Naturally enough, among a hunting people, shooting at a mark was a favorite pastime. The best shot among the pioneers was one who was held in esteem ; and it was refreshing, not many years ago, to see an old man carefully wipe his spectacles and show the boys, in a very convincing way, how much better they could shoot in the good old time than they can now. In Walnut Grove there used to be immense numbers of squirrels, and in the early summer the people, for miles around would collect at the old meeting house spring, on an appointed day, and enjoy what was called a "burgout." A burgout (pronounced burgoo) was a feast, the chief feature of which was squirrel soup. Early on the appointed day the young men would be abroad with rifles, in search of young squirrels. By eight or nine o'clock these would begin to come in from all directions with their game. By this time, the old people and children had gathered together and the work of preparation was begun. Large kettles were suspended over the fire, and in these the dressed squirrels were deliciously souped. By common consent the direction of affairs was surrendered to Uncle "Lijah" Dickinson, who knew exactly how to make the best soup. The young man who brought in the greatest number of squirrels was the hero of the day, and divided the honor, if not the authority with Uncle Lijah. The soup was supplemented by the good things prepared at home, and the feast was always one of bounty and hospitality. It was always held at the old meeting house spring, near the southeast corner of the present college campus, and the memories connected therewith, in many a heart, are pure and sweet as the waters which bubbled up from its depths. Jumping and wrestling were much in fashion, and it was an enviable thing to be the champion in either of these respects. Among indoor sports checkers, fox and geese and hull-gull were very common. Books were scarce, and periodicals rare, while musical instruments were confined chiefly to the violin and accordeon. Croquet and base ball were unknown, but there were bull-pen, town-ball, cat, horseshoe and marbles. These were excellent in their time, but we fear must give place to these new fangled things which are not half so good, you know.

We close this chapter with the impression that change has been, and still is, making rapid inroads upon the manners and customs of our domestic and social life. It stamps itself upon our intercourse and amusements, upon our food and dress, upon our houses and conveniences. Whether those changes are for better or worse will be decided in different ways by different people; but looking over the whole field the conclusion is forced upon us that there has been real progress in all departments of human life. That in the two-fold aspect of individual and social improvement much has been done can hardly be doubted; and the retrospect fills us with hope and high anticipation for our county and mankind.

CHAPTER IV.

AGRICULTURE AND FARM PRODUCTS.

The chief industry among the early settlers of Woodford County was farming. Many of them had been mechanics and tradesmen before emigrating from their old homes, but they found little demand for their services, and soon turned their attention to opening up farms. Almost the whole country is tillable land, and the cultivation of the soil is still the most important interest and is likely to remain so. It will, therefore, be interesting to note the progress of this business during the last fifty years. About the year 1824 some farms were opened in the river bottom, near Spring Bay. About the same time some prairie was broken, on the place now occupied by Joseph Meek, by a man named Joseph Dillon. The first comers either settled in the timber or at the skirts thereof. They knew of the fertility of the prairie land, and the comparative ease with which it could be brought into cultivation, but thought settlements away from the timber would never be possible. They little dreamed that they would live to see these broad prairies one continuous stretch of farms and pleasant homes. They knew little of the treasures of the coal mines under their feet, and less of the wonderful possibilities suggested thereby. The many improved farms on our prairies have chiefly sprung up since the days of coal mines and Chicago pine lumber. Many of the settlers grubbed farms out of the thick trees and brush, at great expense of time and muscle, when thousands of acres of blooming, fertile prairie were in sight of their cabins, unclaimed and unoccupied. The favorite location, however, was at the edge of the timber, where materials for buildings and fences and fuel were at hand, and the farm extended from a half of a mile to a mile into the prairie.

The out-buildings were usually a stable, a corn-crib, a smoke-house and an ash-hopper. The stable, corn-crib and smoke-house were usually of logs, and the ash-hopper of clap-boards. The first frame farm houses were very substantial affairs. The sills, plates and corner posts being heavy, hewed timbers, mortised and pinned together as substantially as the timbers of a modern railroad bridge. Even to this day the old settlers look upon the light, pine frames, now so much in vogue, with a good deal of suspicion. Some of the early barns were buildings of no small pretensions. They were of the solidest materials, and sometimes of considerable size. I remember one which was standing till about the year 1850, on the farm now occupied by Thos. Ray, near Eureka. This building was constructed of logs hewed on two sides, so as to present a smooth wall inside and out. They were about ten inches thick, and some of them, near the base, were not far from three feet broad. The barn was about thirty feet square, and the walls, as I remember them, must have been sixteen feet high, containing in the neighborhood of fifteen thousand feet of hard lumber. The entire space within was occupied by a threshing floor, and triangular grain bins, made by planking off the corners. This threshing floor was made use of by the neighbors generally, before the days of threshing machines. 'They would haul their wheat to the barn in the sheaf, distribute a quantity of it about the center post and then put the horses upon it. After a long time of walking round and round the horses were taken out, the straw raked off and removed, the wheat winnowed by means of shovels, and taken home. The plates of this barn were nicely hewed on four sides, were about ten by eighteen inches and thirty feet long. The raising of such a building must have required the united energies of the whole community.

The oldest plank fences date back only about twenty-five years, and before that time rails were the fencing material. A few fences were made of sod, but these were not common. The splitting and hauling of rails was a work of great labor, but a good rail fence was a substantial and durable affair. In late years the farmers have turned their attention to the growing of hedges, and many experiments have been made with plants of various sorts. The only thing which so far has been generally adopted is the osage orange, a native plant, which grows, under favorable circumstances, to a height of sixty feet. The wood is elastic and fine-grained, and was much used by the Indians for bows. The fruit is about the size and somewhat the appearance of an orange. It has a juicy and wholesome pulp, but is not much relished as an article of food, having an uninviting taste and odor. The scarcity of stone forbids its use as a fencing material.

The early implements of husbandry were of the rudest sort, and the methods slow and laborious. The first plows used in Woodford County were little better than those in use in Asia twenty-five hundred years ago; for they had then wooden plows with iron shares, and these were the only sort known to our fathers fifty years ago. The best plow at that time was the Carey, with wooden mold board, and the cultivator was the old time shovel. Scouring plows were introduced about thirty years ago, and were a great improvement, since they lightened the draft, and, what is equally important, enabled the farmer to turn the crust of the soil upside down, thoroughly pulverizing it, and covering up the weeds. Grain was sowed by hand, and covered by means of harrows or brush drags. Corn was planted by hand and covered with a hoe. Sod corn was planted in every third furrow, and covered by the sod cut by the plow from the next. Corn ground was "laid off" by running furrows with a shovel plow, four feet apart, both ways across the field. This was a tedious process, but for many years it did not occur to any one that a marker might be used, which should make three or four rows at a time. After a time hand planters came to be used, and now we are all familiar with the splendid machines for planting this most important of our products.

Many a young farmer will smile to be told that the crows and blackbirds used to be regarded as formidable enemies of the pioneer's cornfield. These birds were in immense numbers, and cornfields were not numerous nor large, and when the corn was young these thievish imps exhibited great intelligence and commendable industry in pulling it up to get the grain which would adhere to the little stem. It would require several hills of corn to make a breakfast for a hungry blackbird, and they did much mischief in this way. As an offset corn was generally planted too thick, and what the birds failed to thin, had to be thinned by hand, Even at a distance of twenty-five years our back aches at the recollection of that most hated of all pastimes, thinning corn. It was, in our estimation, entirely " too thin." Before the days of double shovels the proper cultivation of corn required three furrows to the row. The older ones would do the plowing next to the rows and leave the boys to " split the middles." Of all the monotonous things in the tedious round and routine of human labor, there is nothing approaching in monotonously monotonous monotony the " splitting of middles." But it has had its day, and has been laid aside with many another tedious thing, which required neither skill nor intelligence but stolid perseverance. At first the harvesting was done largely with the sickle, or reaping hook, but cradles were early introduced. Wheat used to be a much surer crop than at present, and the old-fashioned harvest was a time of plenty in all respects. Plenty of grain, hard work, fun and hot weather. A stout man with a cradle could cut three acres of grain per day, and it is still an open question whether a reaper really saves much time or labor. However, it cannot be doubted that the present inventions of harvesters and self-binders will leave no room for a discussion of this sort. It being impracticable to market grain at all times as now, the wheat and oats were usually stacked and thrashed in the fall and winter. The farms in August presented a cheerful sight, with their green cornfields, golden stubble and huge stackyards. Hay was not so much cultivated as now. Many depended upon wild grasses, and meadows of tame grass occupied only a small portion of the farm. Timothy was the chief tame grass; and sometimes in flat places was a patch of red-top, or English grass, sometimes called herds-grass. After a time clover was introduced and has been found to be useful not only as an article of food for stock, but also for re-fertilizing land which has been exhausted by grain crops. The common red clover is the variety which has been most used. Later claimants for favor, however, have failed to supplant timothy and clover.

For many years hay was cut with the scythe and taken up by hand-rakes and pitchforks; the methods now in use, and the implements for cutting and handling being vastly superior to the old. These render the raising of stock much easier than it could be done without them.

Stock raising was not much of a business in Woodford County before 1850, and has made great progress in the last few years. The first settlers kept a few pigs and cattle in a promiscuous way, with the pastoral idea that they might furnish the family with milk and butter, and meat and lard. The custom of raising and fatting stock for market was unknown. After a time markets were established on the Illinois river for pork, and the farmers began to fatten a few hogs annually. There was no market except in cold weather, and the hogs were all fattened in the fall and winter. Still later a few men began to buy up the odd calves and steers a settler might have, and these were prepared for market, which was either St. Louis or Chicago. Stock raising soon became profitable. It is true pork did not bring much, but it did not cost much to raise hogs. The range was large, and what with wild strawberries, blackberries, and acorns and hazel nuts the pigs would take care of themselves during the summer and fall and come up at the end of the season having outgrown the knowledge of most intimate friends, and ready for easy fattening. Cattle would fatten and grow on the prairies from middle of spring till Christmas, and there was little thought of the time when all this range would be fenced and owned by somebody, and pasturage would be scarce and expensive. We see how that from these rude and careless beginnings the raising of stock has become an important and systematic part of farming. Great improvement has been made in the breeds of cattle and hogs, and our sleek and aristocratic Berkshires, Chesters, Poland-Chinas, Durhams, &c., would hardly claim kin with their ungainly and bony predecessors. Attempts to improve our stock of horses by importations and careful breeding have been frequent in the last few years, and the experiment has not so far advanced as to permit the extent of benefit to be fully determined.

In the matter of poultry, turkeys, chickens, ducks and geese were soon introduced, but there has been great improvement made in chickens. The kinds upon which the pioneer preacher subsisted were tough and poor in comparison with the tender and luscious ones which tempt the modern ministerial palate. The vegetable garden contributed its share to the setler's table. Potatoes, beets, cabbages, onions, beans, peas, and the like, grew in the virgin soil with such cultivation as the women could give them. The chief improvements in these matters being the *early* varieties of such vegetables as have been cultivated from the beginning. Cultivation and experiment have made a gain of from one to two months in the producing of our more important garden vegetables. An advantage not enjoyed by the newcomers is the possibility of getting good and reliable seed. In the old time seeds must be saved from year to year, and new varieties and fresh seeds were hard to get. The garden usually afforded a space for a display of flowers. The kinds were not numerous, but, though old fashioned and of unpretending titles, were beautiful and sweet. It seems that the chief improvement that has been made has been in the matter of names. The beauties which used to gladden our eyes did not rejoice in the high-sounding titles of the modern flower aristocracy. We had no *Dicentra Spectabilis*, no Gladiollus, Gilia Coronopifolia, Passiflora Caerulea, Fuchsia Microphylla, Albizzia Julibrissin. No one can deny that there must be an incalculable amount of beauty, delicacy, rarity and agony which demand such extraordinary verbal exponents, but, as in many other things, it sometimes happens that the magnificence of the name is more easily seen than of the thing named. We are sometimes pervaded with a sense of the ridiculous when we notice some poor, little, misshapen body addressed as your *Majesty*, or some short, dumpy, Esquimau-legged specimen dubbed your *Highness*. But however incongruous the thing must be done, and he is but an uncharitable boor who refuses to see the qualities suggested by these grandiloquent and *appropriate* titles. It is not unusual to see sensible people, neglecting the learned, the beautiful and the truly great, gathering about some scion of effete aristocracy, bowing and scraping, and pretending to admire; nor is it unusual in these days to see sensible young men and women, oblivious to roses and pinks, bestowing care and praise upon some pompously named little weed which has neither grace, elegance nor perfume; and is only recommended by its *name and rarity*. In the good old days there were pinks, and roses, and hollyhocks, and touch-me-nots, and violets, and lilies, and the broad prairies were a vast flower garden themselves. The chief house-plants were such as are sometimes seen in old fashioned families nowadays, and are likely to become of some consideration because of their rarity, although not usually exotic; namely, children. It is worthy of remark that some of the most troublesome pests with which the farmer has to contend, were originally introduced as rare plants and choice flowers by romantic and sentimental cultivators.

The weeds during the first few years of the country did not offer much hinderance to cultivation. The soil was free from noxious seeds, and the farmer could tend with his single plow, forty or fifty acres of corn; and it seems that the improvement in cultivators has not been more than sufficient to counterbalance the increasing crops of weeds. New sorts are constantly met with, and many a farmer is coming to the conclusion that he has been trying to cultivate too much ground, until his land is foul with all manner of villainous growth. Fewer acres to the hand and more thorough and repeated attacks seems to be the only remedy.

We have seen that fifty years have made a marvelous change in nearly everything pertaining to agriculture in Woodford County. Some of these changes have been for the better, some for the worse, but that the direction has been such that we may call the whole movement a progress cannot be denied. We may safely say there has been a great and gratifying improvement. In comfort and independence, in security of person and property, in social and political importance, in moral worth and respectability and downright enjoyment of the best gifts of Nature, there is probably no people in the world which surpasses the farmers of Woodford County.

CHAPTER V.

MANUFACTURES, TRADE, ETC.

Woodford County has not made the same progress in manufactures as in other branches of industry. About fifty years ago mills for the preparation of flour and meal began to be thought of, but most of the necessary articles were made at home. Indian corn was pounded in a mortar dug out of a stump or trunk of a tree. This was a slow and laborious process. In a few years horse mills were established, by means of which wheat was ground. The flour was sifted and bolted by hand. Gradually improved machinery and methods have been introduced, until grades of flour are produced equal to those anywhere in the world. This bracnh of business has suffered much in the last ten years because of the almost constant failure of the wheat crop in Central Illinois.

Iron manufacture has never flourished to any extent among us. Blacksmiths' shops were early needed for the repairing of vehicles, shoeing of horses, making of nails and supplying other needed articles, but beyond something of this sort little has been done to the present time. We have had our boot and shoe makers from the beginning, and good mechanics of this class are to be found in all of our towns, but there is nothing in the shape of a manufactory of this sort in our county. In the making of wagons and carriages we have a little better showing, and in several places considerable capital and skill are at present employed. As we have seen, the manufacture of fabrics was at one time an extensive domestic industry, but it seems never to have got beyond the limits of home. We have no establishment for the manufacture of cloths, and perhaps the nearest approach to it are the semi-domestic factories of traditional rag carpet.

Without being more specific in details, we may state briefly some of the causes which have hindered the growth of the county in the above respect. In the first place labor and capital have found ready employment in agriculture and trade, which have seemed to offer surer and speedier returns. In time past factories have seemed to flourish best where agriculture flourished least, and the energy of the people turned into the channel of manufacturing only when denied any other. This fact often separated the factory and the product upon which it operated by wide distances. It put the cotton mills in Massachusetts and England, hundreds or thousands of miles away from the staple upon which they feed. We are beginning to find that this is putting asunder what God has joined together. If Woodford County can produce wool it is but reasonable to suppose that she can manufacture that wool into cloths, and make it profitable. If we can produce excellent and abundant broom corn, we can produce excellent brooms in immense quantities, and it will be wise for us to look about to see if there be not some of these complementary industries to which we can turn our hands. Instead of making endless failures in spring wheat it would be better to raise flax, and then operate factories that would utilize both the fiber and the seed. That our county is well adapted to agriculture will probably be seen to be the very reason why it is well adapted to certain sorts of manufacture; but curiously enough these are the very sorts that have received least attention.

Another reason assigned for our slow progress in manufactures is the scarcity of fuel, but immense coal deposits have recently been developed upon two sides of us, and the very best bituminous coal can be had by deep mining, at any point in our territory. Besides there is much difference in the amount of fuel required to carry on the different sorts of factories, and those manufactures of which we produce the raw material in greatest abundance require comparatively little fuel.

The first settlers had but little money of any sort, and but little chance of getting more. It used to be that letters were paid for at the place of delivery, and sometimes, if the letters came far, the sum would amount to twenty-five cents in silver. I have been told by those who know, that a settler would often be compelled to wait from a week to a month before he could scrape up enough money to get his mail. This sounds like extravagant talk, but there is the best of reason for believing that many among us, who are now wealthy farmers, were often put to such straits as these. At first whatever was raised in the way of grain, over and above the needs of the family and the new immigrants, was permitted to waste, there being no market. Pretty soon, however, a market for grain and stock was established at Fort Clark (Peoria), and then at Spring Bay. Pork would sell from a dollar and a quarter to a dollar and a half per hundred weight, dressed, wheat about three bits a bushel, and corn for almost nothing. They were usually paid for in high priced goods and paper money.

This money was of the most doubtful character, and the settler never knew whether it would be worth anything when he wanted to use it. The hardy pioneers of our civilization did not sit down and whine over these hardships, but were wide awake and took every advantage of circumstances. If they could do a little better at Pekin, some one would be sure to find it out and tell his neighbors, and if the market should drop there they would go to Peoria, or even away off to Chicago Many a load of grain has been hauled the latter distance from our county, and hogs have been driven to the same market, in the rigors of winter. The distance which produce had to be hauled, and the lack of information with respect to the markets, left little room for the exercise of discretion and foresight in the disposal of a crop. The farmer would hear that a good price was being paid for wheat in Peoria, or Spring Bay, and would quickly clean up a load and put for market. But he was often too late, and the market had broken down. I was told by an old settler that once, in a very dull time, he took a load of wheat to Pekin. To his surprise and delight he received fifty cents a bushel, and that too, in bright silver. With great joy he returned home and hastily prepared another load to be taken next day, meanwhile sending the good news to his neighbors. The news spread rapidly, and the next morning our settler put out with his load for Pekin. But imagine his chagrin when he discovered that the market had fallen nearly one half, and the only money being paid out was the doubtfullest sort of "shinplasters." He was compelled to dispose of his wheat thus, and in different mood from the day before, wended his way home as the evening shadows gathered about him. But all this time the news had been traveling, and he met teams from away east of Panther Creek, hurrying wheat to Pekin to get the silver half dollar per bushel. It seems that some of the early grain buyers in certain " ways " and "tricks" resembled the "heathen Chinee," very closely.

By and by things began to improve. By 1830 steamboats began to ascend the Illinois river, and take produce from Pekin, Peoria and Spring Bay, to St. Louis and New Orleans, In 1840 Munn & Scott established themselves in Spring Bay as grain buyers and general merchants, and trade was divided between Chicago and the points below. The opening of the Illinois and Michigan Canal was a great step for the commerce of Wooford County, and when the Central Railroad was completed in 1852 we began to feel assured of our future. Since that time new roads have been built, and markets and places of trade have been established within easy reach in all parts of the county. Unforeseen circumstances have brought our pioneers, who used to wonder what disposition they could ever make of the products of their rich soil, to the very door of the greatest grain and stock market upon the globe.

These changes have not only brought markets to ou

door, but with them have brought accurate daily information of markets all over the country. A settler on the prairie in Roanoke township to-day, can know more of the markets in New York and Liverpool yesterday, than he could have known forty years ago of the markets of Peoria and Spring Bay the day before. Postal privileges, which were formerly scarce and costly, are now enjoyed to the full and at but little cost. Our first settlers had to get their mail from Peoria and Mackinawtown, and these places were far away from many of them. After a time post offices were established at Washington, Metamora, &c., and the settlers felt that with a post office within ten miles and mail every week things were getting handy. If we could drop our daily mails and daily newspapers and go back thirty years we should have a better realization of the disadvantages with which our fathers and mothers had to contend, if we should be compelled to give up no other conveniences than these.

Goods began to be sold at Spring Bay, Metamora, Versailles and Bowling Green, and for many years these were places of considerable trade. Not many fine goods were brought, and such as were for common use were sold at high prices. It sometimes happens that a bushel of wheat will buy a calico dress, but in the olden time a bushel of wheat would often fail to pay for a single yard. Ten bushels of corn would often be thought a good price for a pair of boots, but our early settlers often saw the time when a team couldn't carry enough corn to market to secure one pair of stogas. There has been great improvement, not only in prices, but in the quality and variety of commodities sold, and in the matter of general merchandise it seems that an unrestrained competition has had its full and legitimate effect. It is probable, as hinted above, that this business has been overdone in this county. There are too many merchants and clerks and not enough manufacturers and working men, and it seems that there is a substantial reward awaiting the prudent investment of capital in suitable industries. With all her resources developed, and all her energies wisely directed, Woodford County will be the home of an intelligent, healthy and happy people.

CHAPTER VI.

POLITICS, LAW AND MEDICINE.

The citizens of Woodford County have always taken much interest in politics, and political gatherings and speech-making have been customary for many years. Up to the formation of the Republican party in 1856 the two prominent parties were Whig and Democrat, but the Democrats were in considerable majority. There were a few citizens, living chiefly above Metamora, who possessed an intense hatred to southern slavery, and did not respect the Fugitive Slave Law. Investigation before the grand jury showed, that in all probability, there existed in this vicinity one of what were called "the stations of the underground railroad." These were nothing more nor less than hiding places for fugitive slaves who were trying to make their way to Canada. The stations would be at convenient distances, such as could be driven or walked in a night, and the fugitives would travel in the darkness, and find concealment, shelter and provisions during the day at the hands of people who thought they were doing right in thus defeating a cruel and unjust law. It seems that there was a station in Tazewell county, one in Woodford and one in Bureau county, connecting with others north and south, forming a continuous line from the slave states to Canada. There existed many such lines as these running through the northern states, and many a poor negro followed them to liberty. The existence of this station soon became known to the citizens of the county, but many did not seem to wish to interfere, and had little inclination to wrest the captive from the hands of his helpers and send him back to slavery. Some, however, regarded them as law-breakers, and much prejudice was stirred up, and at times excitement ran very high. I believe, however, that little or no violence was ever resorted to in Woodford County on this account.

Since 1856 the two prominent parties have been the Democratic and Republican. The Democrats have always been in the majority, and have usually controlled the county offices. When the rebellion broke out in 1861, with but few exceptions, political questions were made of secondary importance, and our county was among the first to furnish troops for the preservation of the Union. From the best information it seems that, first and last, we furnished about fifteen hundred soldiers to the Union armies, being fully one-tenth of the entire population. There was little or no public disturbance among the people during the war, and I think it may be truthfully said that Woodford County bore her full share of the terrible burden with patience and cheerfulness.

During political campaigns immense open air meetings have been customary in our county, and our citizens are familiar with the oratory of Lincoln and Douglas, and Trumbull, and Allen, and Yates, and Dickey, and Ingersoll, and scores of others prominent in the political world.

About twenty years ago the American party had organization and a good many adherents in many parts of the county, but I believe it does not exist as a separate organization at present; although there are those who still advocate the principles and doctrines which it then advocated. Prohibition has figured to some extent of late years as a political issue in the county but has never succeeded in controlling elections to any extent. The Temperance party in 1869 seemed to possess more vigor and shape politically than since, not, perhaps, because our citizens are indifferent as regards the matter, but because the prominent political organizations have not been willing to regard temperance as a legitimate political issue. There was as early as 1851, at Metamora, a society known as "Division 33, Sons of Temperance, of the State of Illinois," with printed Constitution and Bylaws and Rules of Order. About 1856 a large public meeting was held in the Christian church in Walnut Grove and strong resolutions against the liquor traffic were prepared and generally signed.

The Democrats and Republicans have been represented for a number of years by party newspapers, the Democratic located at Metamora, "The Woodford *Sentinel*," and the Republican, the "*Journal*," at El Paso. In 1854 there was put forth, by C. McKinzie, a prospectus for the "Woodford County *Times*," to be devoted to news and politics. It was to be Democratic. I believe this was the beginning of newspaper enterprises among us. Metamora long enjoyed the preeminence of being the only place of publication in the county. In the year 1865 the "El Paso *Journal*" was commenced, and in the year 1867 the "Eureka *Journal.*" The newspapers of the county at present are the "*Sentinel,*" Metamora; the "*Journal,*" El Paso; the "*Journal,*" Eureka, and the "*Times,*" Minonk.

The early administration of justice, of course, partook somewhat of the irregularities and peculiarities characteristic of this art in all new countries Justice is a goddess who possesses wonderful powers of adaptation to circumstances, and makes her abode with the rude backwoodsmen as contentedly as with the learned and wealthy. Among our fathers the best facilities for punishing crime were not always afforded, and sometimes it happened in new countries that the friends of law and order are in the minority. It so happened in some portions of Illinois. Probably the most impudent defiers of the law, and those who most provoked the wrath of the settlers, were horse thieves. These fellows occasionally coupled with their regular vocation, by way of variety, burglary and highway robbery. There existed, no doubt, throughout the west a numerous and organized band of these desperate villains. They seem to have got the start of the law, and sometimes secured the election of members of the gang to local offices. To counteract these dangers the early settlers united in an organization known as the " Regulators." These often made short and unceremonious work of horse thieves and robbers. Our county suffered considerably from these depredators, but our citizens never found the opposition to law strong enough to resort to lynch law.

Among the early settlers legal knowledge and advice was not always attainable, but the juctices and officers were usually men of great practical sense, and undoubted integrity. Their methods of getting at truth and fairness were sometimes excentric and original, but it is probable that equal and exact justice was done as often as by our present more refined, technical and involved processes. Lawyers were scarce, and suits were sometimes disposed of in a way which might provoke a professional smile, but somehow it all averaged well, and the majesty of the law was vindicated and maintained. Even after the organization of the county, and the circuit court brought in such men as Lincoln, S. T. Logan and Davis, there was a free and easy way about courts and lawyers which would be refreshing if it could be revived at present. While Judge Treat was presiding at Versailles he would frequently summon the lawyers from their contests with the settlers in jumping and horse-shoe pitching to attend to their business indoors. The officer would sometimes find Lincoln at these sports, with coat off and full of excitement, when needed in court. In those days the court room was the scene of the utmost good humor and hilarity. Jokes and anecdotes were current, and attending court, in the days of my boyhood, was better than a circus. The same spirit has not always characterized our legal proceedings, and I have witnessed in our county some disgusting and humiliating spectacles of bullying, brow-beating and abuse. It is believed, however, that this is a thing of the past, and that our bar is at present characterized by a higher tone. Without attempting to blame any one in particular, it is well for the fraternity to see to it that coarseness and profanity

H

shall never again become so prevalent as formerly.

For a long time after the removal of the county seat nearly the whole bar resided at Metamora, but lawyers are found at present in all parts of the county. The first licensed attorney was John B. Holland, who went to California in 1849, and died there. Prominent among those who have first and last expounded the law in our midst, and taught our people the eternal principles of justice, are S. P. Shope, Welcome P. Brown, C. H. Chitty, John Clark, R. T. Cassell. A. E. Stevenson, Briggs and Meek, E. D. Davidson, Harper and Cassell and a lot of younger men whose names will probably figure in history by and by.

But it is time now that we should turn our attention to another important class of men, the need of which is felt in all communities, whether barbarous or civilized— the medical fraternity. Communities feel the need of and appreciate the doctor long before the lawyer, the pedagogue or even the preacher. Among rude people the "Medicine Man" shares the honor with the Chief, and the dignity and authority of both offices are often blended in the same individual; while among civilized and polished communities there is no more useful or respected man than the competent and conscientious physician.

The prevalent diseases among the early settlers were remittent, or intermittent, fevers in the late summer and fall, and pneumonia in the winter. Against the first there seemed to be no adequate means of defense. The immense quantity of vegetation exposed to the heat and moisture as the summer advanced produced miasma in such quantities that no locality escaped. It would sometime happen that not a single family in a settlement would be free from malarial affections, and often whole families would be stricken down with ague, and no one able to care for the others. In this condition they would be cared for by the neighbors, and many acts of kindness and self-sacrifice thus called out are remembered by the old settlers with lively pleasure. If the present generation has wherein to boast over the last, it is not in the matter of hospitality or good Samaritanism.

At first the settlers were compelled to depend upon their own knowledge and resources in combatting disease. Now and then a man would couple with his farming the healing art, and some of these, by observation and experience, acquired a considerable degree of skill, and were usually regarded as oracles by the neighbors. Sometimes this office would be assumed by some old lady, who, combining a little experience, good sense and superstition with a deal of good nursing and encouragement, often succeeded marvelously. Inasmuch as these practitioners usually gave their services for nothing, and enjoyed the confidence of the people, the early physicians found it difficult to get a foothold. There was another fact, however, which made it hard for the first regular practitioners. The people of the county had largely imbibed the doctrine of Dr. Samuel Thomson, and they looked with much suspicion and prejudice upon these "Old School" or "Calomel" doctors. Dr. Thomson taught that since minerals were derived from the depths of the earth, their use would drag the patient down into the grave; but that vegetable medicines would raise the body up, inasmuch as it is the nature of vegetables to spring up from the ground. Disease was attacked by means of such weapons as lobelia, cayenne pepper, coffee, number-six, steaming and sweating. Those fellows who gave calomel and let blood and drew blisters were regarded with some distrust if not aversion.

It was, perhaps, as well when each family had to keep its own medicines and often to administer them by guess, that the nostrums were of such character, instead of more potent drugs, which might have done infinitely more harm. But so deeply do prejudices relative to the healing art take hold of people that they are with difficulty overcome. I think some of the old settlers would almost as soon have died according to Thomsonianism as to have recovered under the ministration of calomel, etc. Things are changed now, and lobelia no longer claims authority to set up its rule in every disordered stomach, and will no longer cure all maladies. But to return to the doctors.

The first regular physician among us was Dr. Hazzard, who settled near Germantown in 1836. After eleven years of usefulness he was thrown from his buggy and killed. Dr. Wm. C. Anthony, another regularly educated physician, located at Bowling Green in 1837, but left soon after the county was organized. "Medicine men" of this sort did not accumulate very rapidly, and the next one did not put in an appearance until 1846. At that date Dr. J. S. Whitmire, then a young man, took up his abode at Metamora, and for more than thirty years has waged a successful and unrelenting warfare against the diseases which beset our frail tabernacles, in all parts of the county. A little more than a year afterward came Dr. R. B. M. Wilson, but he soon removed to Washington, Tazewell county, where he has since resided. Although not a resident of our county he, as well as Dr. G. P. Wood, was a frequent visitor at the households of our early settlers. Among those who have combatted the ills to which flesh is heir, may be found the name of A. Reynolds, who pioneered the way against Thomsonianism about Bowling Green, beginning his campaign in 1848. Dr. J. G. Zeller was one of the first physicians in the western part of the county, where he is still in successful practice. There were some physicians of the eclectic school among us, some years ago, who practiced with considerable success. Among these were Richard Bard, of Versailles, and Drs. Springgate and Tandy, of Eureka. The eclectics are still represented by Dr. Maloney, of Washburn, and Dr. J. M. John, of Roanoke.

In 1870 was organized the Woodford County Medical Society, which holds frequent sessions for the advancement of medical science, and the discussion of questions connected with the profession. In this association no one is admitted to membership except those who have received a diploma from some medical institution authorized to confer degrees. The present membership is as follows: Drs. Whitmire and Kinnear, Metamora; Cole and Lamme, El Paso; Crawford, Lichtenberger and Rosenberg, Eureka; Blanchard, Minonk; Morgan and Wilkinson, Roanoke; Slemmons, Benson; Darling, Low Point; Garrett, Newkirk and Tweddale, Washburn; Dr. Gill. Prominent among the fraternity is Dr. Wilcox, of Minonk, who has found opportunity to engage to some extent in politics, with success; and Dr Z. H. Whitmire, who was for many years in partnership with his brother, at Metamora.

CHAPTER VII.

EDUCATIONAL AND RELIGIOUS MATTERS.

Great progress has been made by us in educational matters. The first school of which I can find any trace was kept in a little log hut near where E. B. Myers afterward settled. It was in the year 1832. Not long afterwards Joshua Woosley taught near the head of the grove. About the same time, away over in White Oak, on the place now owned by Winton Carlock, old Abner Peeler began the training of the backwoods youth. A little later still, down in the Uncle Jimmy Harlan neighborhood, intellectual culture was attempted, and this time by a lady. Mary Ann Brown heads the list of educators of Montgomery township. Somewhere about 1835 the settlers on Ten Mile, in the western part, erected a school house, and George Hopkins undertook the arduous task of instilling through eye and ear and spine the rudiments of learning. This was one of the first school houses, and lest our youngsters should get a wrong notion of it I will attempt a description of the primitive school house. It was nearly square and built of logs. For light a log was left out of one side. The opening was sometimes converted into a " window " by being filled with greased paper for glass Again it would be filled by a broad board, which being let down upon pegs upon the inside, answered for writing desk. Writing could only be attended to when the window was open, and if it was cold or windy there must have been some attendant inconvenience. At one end of the room was a fireplace which had a lively, cheerful air in winter, when it was put to its best to keep out the cold, but had a dreary, vacant goneness about it in summer. Of all the sad, fancy-smothering, regretful things an old-fashioned, gaping fireplace, with its black, sooty jambs and funereal ashes and idle dog-irons is the chief. Housewives used to fill them up with boughs of trees and asparagus bushes, or something of that sort, before screens were thought of. But nobody attempted to relieve the desolation of the school house fireplace. Like a ruin in the wilderness or a carcass upon the plain it was left to its lonesomeness. A stove looks like something, even when not in use, but an unused fireplace is a great yawning emptiness. But we were talking about the old time school houses. The benches consisted of a rough slab with four rude pins, and required no other tools in their construction than an ax and big auger. Maps, charts, globes and blackboards were unknown, and the searchers after knowledge had few helps in their tasks; nor even many comforts. If one of our modern teachers should be thrust into such surroundings with his work he would be apt to abandon the field in utter defeat. And yet the pioneers in education wrought patiently and successfully through all these disadvantages and laid well the foundation of learning and intelligence in our midst.

The first school about Spring Bay was kept in the house of Benjamin Williams, by a man named Ellmore, and the first school in Partridge was taught by Mary Curry. A sort of itinerant school was taught at Low Point, in 1837, by Miss Love Morse. It was kept one week at the house of James Owen and the next at the house of Parker Morse. Miss Morse kept a schedule of attendance at the school, and the expenses were paid out of the state treasury, according to the record. This was probably the first free school ever taught in northern Illinois.

There were many trials and difficulties in the way of the early pedagogue which the modern one does not encounter. One of these was the necessity of boarding around. Hash was more abundant than money, and when the settler subscribed for a scholar, scholar and a half, or two scholars, or any other number, he stipulated to pay part of the price by boarding the "ma'am" or "master." By a curious law this would throw the teacher most of the time into the most unpleasant quarters. If a family was large, the same cause which would furnish many pupils and require the pedagogue to board longer with the family would also leave little room for his accommodation. By this plan, however, the teacher became familiar with all sorts of people, accommodations, fare, houses and all degrees of cleanliness, and what he lost in comfort and convenience he gathered up in experience. He had good opportunity to acquire that facility of adaptation to circumstances—the becoming all things to all men—which contribute so largely to success in any calling; and the chances to study all species of the genus homo in their native haunts was most excellent. Another trial was the in-

I

subordination of the pupils. Muscle was a thing much relied on in those early days, and the successful teacher must be able to thrash the biggest boy in school, or his authority was constantly in danger. Pluck and generalship were necessary qualities. Holidays were not granted, as now, by legal enactment, nor upon formal petition, but by forcible expulsion of the master from the school house. They were days of time-honored mutiny and legitimate rebellion, which threatened to extend to all the other days of the calendar. All honor to the heroes who maintained their ground on these doubtful battle-fields. Among these honored ones of the long ago will be found the names of Noel Merk, Sr., E. D. Perrin, the wonderful scribe, A. B. Cram, Holcomb Robbins and many others; but probably he who has battled longest and most successfully in the cause of education in Woodford County is A. S. Fisher, who has persistently worked in this field for nearly thirty years.

When we turn from the state of affairs described above to contemplate the present condition of educational matters in our midst, it seems almost incredible that all this change should have been wrought in a single generation. But so it is. In almost every village and rural district we find the neat and painted school house, and the trained teacher, who is beginning already to regard his work as a profession. He takes some educational periodical, attends institutes and appreciates the necessity of study and experiment in himself. Our large towns have their graded schools and tasteful and imposing structures. Great credit is due especially to El Paso and Metamora for the excellent buildings and facilities which they have provided for the public schools. We commend their example to other places. This advice will not be received, of course, by those who regard the money, paid in school taxes, almost thrown away; but will not be lost upon that better class who think mental training one of the necessaries of life, and cheap at whatever cost of mere dollars. Although so much has been done in the last generation in the way of public education, we have not yet arrived at the quitting place, and there is room for as much to be done in the next generation. Too many of our teachers still regard their work as simply a temporary employment, and not a profession to be held fast for life. Men cannot achieve success with this idea in law, medicine, commerce or agriculture, nor can they in teaching. Institutes should meet with more encouragement and awaken more interest, not specially on the part of the public authorities, but on the part of the teachers themselves and the people generally. They are not only essential to the development of the best ideas and methods relative to the work of teaching, but are the best promoters of that fellowship which the French call *esprit de corps*, so necessary to the success of any army, whether of soldiers, teachers or Christians. We need public libraries and museums, not hidden away in colleges and seminaries where they only benefit the student, but they should be thrown in the way of the public and maintained at public expense.

With respect to the higher collegiate education Woodford County has no mean record, and can boast of as honest an effort in this direction as any county in the state. Much remains to be done, however, in this behalf. Many persons not only fail to sustain and encourage the higher culture, but utterly fail to understand what it is. There is a cheap imitation of gentility in dress and manner which passes for the genuine article among certain sorts of people, but is ridiculous and disgusting to persons of real refinement. This counterfeit gentility is found as often among the rich as the poor, and is as plainly visible under silk and broadcloth as homespun. In like manner there is a cheap imitation of higher education, or collegiate culture. It is *cheap* because it is secured at little outlay of time or labor, and is worth just about as much as it costs. There is a sort of shallow *normalism* which insists that two or three years are about all that can be profitably given to culture, in the period of youth. There are many so called "normal schools" in the land which profess to do for a young man, in two or three years, what our colleges cannot do in less than five or six. This is sheer pretense and deception, and its effects are being seen in the weak and shallow mentality of many of our "educated" men. But Woodford County has done something for that patient and thorough development of the intellectual and moral faculties which deserves the name of higher education. There are many who recognize youth as a period of growth in intellectual and moral faculties, and that cultivation ought to correspond with the whole period of growth. A farmer might as well attempt to cultivate his corn by working it three days, as the educator attempt to train and cultivate men in two or three years. Friends of education ought to begin to understand that the *time* of cultivation cannot be shortened without detriment to mental growth and strength.

Impressed with the necessity of thorough education some men about Walnut Grove, under the leadership of Ben. Major, about 1850, inaugurated the Walnut Grove Seminary, with A. S. Fisher, principal, and Miss Susan Jones, assistant. This soon developed into the "Walnut Grove Academy," and in February, 1855, secured a charter from the State legislature under the name of "Eureka College," with the following Board of Trustees: Elijah Dickinson, Wm. Davenport, E. B. Myers, John Durst, John Lindsey, A. M. Myers, John Major, W. H. Davenport, B. J. Radford, David Deweese, R. M. Clark, Wm. Atteberry, Wm. T. Major, C. O. Neville, John Bennett, Wm. M. Brown, Jno. T. Jones, Wm. S. Pickerell, Geo. McManus, Bushrod W. Henry, I. T Logan, P. C. Redding, Henry Grove and Jno. W. Taylor. This institution has been in constant and successful operation ever since the above date, and has instructed, for shorter or longer periods, over three thousand pupils, more than half of whom have come from other counties. The college is still flourishing and has a corps of eight experienced instructors, and ranks among the first institutions of its class in the state.

Recently a movement was made to establish an academy at Low Point. Funds were secured and a neat and commodious frame building was erected, well adapted to the wants of the young institution. Prof. J. E. Lamb was appointed principal, and the academy soon got well under way, but an unforeseen calamity was in store for it. A few months since the building was burned to the ground, and by some strange oversight there had been no insurance provided. As soon as they recovered a little from the blow the friends of the enterprise began to think of rebuilding, and money was subscribed, but the hard times make the work drag, and the issue seems somewhat doubtful. The people of Low Point cannot well afford to let this matter fall through, and ought to resurrect the institution at whatever sacrifice. A grand stride will have been taken by our people in the march of civilization when they become willing to expend as much upon the brain as the stomach, and come to recognize food for the mind as among the necessaries of life. Let every citizen of Woodford County hasten the time.

If the people of Woodford are not, like the ancient Athenians, exceedingly religious, they are by no means to be reckoned as heathens. The voice of the preacher of the gospel was heard in the cabins of the early settlers, and in the groves which were lately the haunts of the Red man and the panther. About 1829 a Presbyterian minister came to Walnut Grove. He was invited to preach at a settler's cabin, but soon after the sermon began two of the boys got into a fisticuff pastime. Services were interrupted until the disturbances were quieted, when the preacher proceeded. This was, perhaps, the earliest voice in the wilderness of these parts, but not many Presbyterian ministers came this way for a long while, and it was not until 1868 that a Presbyterian church was organized at Eureka. In 1841 Rev. W. T. Adams, now of El Paso, preached at Low Point in the house of Mr. Farnsworth, but no church was organized here until 1853. At that time some fourteen members were gathered together, constituted a congregation and enjoyed the ministry of Wm. P. Carson. Wm. Dodds was first elder. The present membership is nearly one hundred. There was organized the next year, 1854, another church known as United Presbyterians, which is in a prosperous condition at present. In 1856 Wm. Frost began to preach at Minonk, and the next year organized a Presbyterian church at this point. The first organization of this denomination at Metamora was in 1858; and their first minister was I. A. Cornelison. It began with a small membership. Mr. Cornelison, in 1868, gathered together some twenty-four members at Eureka and organized them into a church, and they soon secured the services of Rev. Samuel Hart, under whose care they prospered. They now have an elegant house of worship and are thriving under the ministry of Rev. M. P. Ormsby. The Presbyterian church in El Paso was organized by W. T. Adams in 1857. Mr. Adams became the pastor in 1864. The congregation is now large and prosperous.

Methodism early gained a firm foothold among the settlers in Woodford County. The first church erected on Ten Mile was Methodist, and the preacher's name was Lattey. He was followed by Uncle Zedick Hall, the famous pioneer Methodist preacher. Father Hall has been a zealous teacher of religion in our county and surrounding regions for more than two score years, and is still vigorous and enthusiastic. He preached throughout Central Illinois in the early day, encountering with much fortitude the dangers and hardships incident to his work, and has done as much, perhaps, to build up righteousness and temperance as any man among us. He resides with his son in Worth township. About 1840 Jeter Foster began preaching about Low Point and soon built up a Methodist church at that place. They erected a meeting house here in 1851. Among the early planters of Methodism in Walnut Grove was Uncle Jimmy Wells, and in almost every neighborhood was to be found the Methodist preacher and exhorter, so that these people are numerous and found in almost all parts of the county. They have congregations in all the principal towns and neighborhoods.

The Baptists were among the first to proclaim the gospel among us. It is said the first sermon ever preached about Low Point was by a Baptist named A. M. Root at the house of Isaac Buckingham. The Missionary Baptists built a church here in 1846 on the farm now owned by S. Mundell. But the first Baptist church organized in the county was in the south-eastern part at the house of Jas. Vance. This was done by J. D. Newell in the year 1837, and the congregation consisted of about a dozen members. Soon afterward, in Cazenovia, the old Richland Baptist church was organized. The church at Minonk was organized about 18 years ago, and has been under the pastoral care of Rev. C. D. Merrit ever since. The Baptists have at present, in the county, eleven organizations and about one thousand members, and expend annually for church and benevolent purposes above ten thousand dollars.

The Christian church was represented among the early settlers by a number of preachers among whom were John Oatman, Abner Peeler, Henry D. Palmer, Jas. Robeson, Wm. Davenport and Jas. Owen. By the efforts of these men congregations of Disciples were established in nearly all parts of the county. There are at present eleven organizations with a membership of above twelve hundred. Their two veteran preachers are John T. Jones, of Eureka, aged 82, and James Robeson, of Secor, aged 80. Father Robeson, familiarly known as "Uncle Jimmy," is still vigorous and preaches regularly, having been a preacher of the gospel about sixty years. The denomination has done much for education in the county, having built and sustained Eureka College; although the Methodists and Presbyterians of Eureka have liberally assisted them in their commendable work.

Besides the above denominations there are several smaller religious organizations of somewhat later origin. There is a prosperous congregation of Tunkers, or German Baptists, near Roanoke, and there are two congregations of Omish, or Amish, among us These latter are a portion of the great Mennonite denomination. The Catholics have also organized in several parts of the county, though we have no statistics respecting them.

Probably the first Sunday school in this county was organized by Father Morse, in 1837, at his house in Low Point. Gradually the necessity and fitness of Sunday schools was perceived by religious teachers of all sorts, and all denominations came to regard them as an excellent means of religious training. In all our towns and many country churches good Sunday schools are maintained, and it is probable that some two thousand children receive regular instruction by this means. A fact which is full of hope for the Christian and philanthropist.

Neighbor, here we bid you good bye. We have seen that in the fifty years since Woodford County was first settled by white men, there has been a wonderful improvement in all matters pertaining to physical comfort and conveniences ; to intellectual and social life, to moral and religious institutions and agencies. We have been rapidly catching up with, and finding our place in, the great march of civilization in older communities, but there remains much for all of us to do. He is the best citizen who appreciates most fully and promotes most zealously the improvement of his fellow men in all respects—physical, intellectual and moral. Let us quit ourselves like men. Woodford County, desirable as it may be, can only be ours for a little time, and it would be well for us to secure a claim where homesteads never change hands, and there are no graveyards on the hill sides.

www.ingramcontent.com/pod-product-compliance
Lightning Source LLC
Chambersburg PA
CBHW020335090426
42735CB00009B/1542